# Toys I play with

## Rainy days

Barbara Hunter

Heinemann
LIBRARY

Little Nippers

**www.heinemann.co.uk/library**
Visit our website to find out more information about **Heinemann Library** books.

To order:
 Phone 44 (0) 1865 888066
 Send a fax to 44 (0) 1865 314091
Visit the Heinemann Bookshop at www.heinemann.co.uk/library to browse our catalogue and order online.

First published in Great Britain by Heinemann Library, Halley Court, Jordan Hill, Oxford OX2 8EJ, part of Harcourt Education.
Heinemann is a registered trademark of Harcourt Education Ltd.

Editorial: Jilly Attwood and Claire Throp
Design: Jo Hinton-Malivoire and bigtop, Bicester, UK
Models made by: Jo Brooker
Picture Research: Catherine Bevan
Production: Lorraine Warner

Originated by Dot Gradations
Printed and bound in China by South China Printing Company

ISBN 0 431 16342 1 (hardback)
06 05 04 03 02
10 9 8 7 6 5 4 3 2 1

ISBN 0 431 16347 2 (paperback)
06 05 04 03 02
10 9 8 7 6 5 4 3 2 1

**British Library Cataloguing in Publication Data**
Hunter, Barbara
Rainy days. – (Toys I play with)
790.1'33
A full catalogue record for this book is available from the British Library.

**Acknowledgements**
The publishers would like to thank the following for permission to reproduce photographs:
Alvey and Towers pp. **6**, **16**, **18**, **19**; Bubbles p. **7a** (Pauline Cutler); Collections p. **15** (Peter Wright); Sally & Richard Greenhill Photo Library p. **10** (Sally Greenhill), p. **20-21** (Richard Greenhill); Sylvia Cordaiy Photo Library p. **17** (Humphrey Evans); Tografox pp. **4-5**, **7b**, **8**, **9**, **11**, **12-13**, **14** (R. D. Battersby).

Cover photograph reproduced with permission of Gareth Boden.

The publishers would like to thank Annie Davy for her assistance in the preparation of this book.

Every effort has been made to contact copyright holders of any material reproduced in this book. Any omissions will be rectified in subsequent printings if notice is given to the publishers.

# Contents

# Games and puzzles

Games and puzzles are good
to play with when it rains.

You have to fit all the shapes in the right place to finish this puzzle. Can you see what the shapes are?

# Potato prints

Can you make a painting using potatoes?

What colour paints can
you see here?

squish

squish

7

wooden bricks

8

plastic bricks

Can you guess what
this boy is building?

**Reading**

Reading is fun to do when it is raining outside.

Some cars can go very **FAST** down a ramp.

beep
beep

An electric train can go really
fast, round and round the track.

13

## Dens

It is fun to make your own den when it is wet outside.

# What would you use to make a den?

# Toy animals

# Which animals would you like to play with on a rainy day?

# Making cakes

Cakes can be good to make when it rains.

You might need some help making them and eating them!

# Rockets

Can you make a rocket out of a cardboard box?

Where will you pretend to go in it?

whoosh!

# Actions

painting

building

reading

making

23

# Index

The end

## Notes for adults

This series supports the young child's knowledge and understanding of their world. The following Early Learning Goals are relevant to the series.
• Find out about, and identify, some features of living things, objects and events that they observe.
• Exploration and investigation: feeling textures and materials.

The series explores a range of different play experiences by looking at features of different toys and the materials they are made from. **Rainy Days** includes things made from the following materials: cardboard, paper, wood, plastic, metal, fabric, glass, and porcelain. Some of the experiences featured in this book include being in a limited space, and playing both alone and with a partner.

There is an opportunity for the child to compare and contrast different toys as well as relating them to their own experiences. Many of the play experiences may be familiar to the child but others will provide the opportunity to talk about and perhaps try new ones.

### Follow-up activities
By making direct reference to the book the child can be encouraged to try new experiences such as the following: making cakes, doing a jigsaw, making a den. Taking photographs of the activities would be an excellent way for the child to start making their own book.